MISS? WE DON'T REALLY...

A STEP AHEAD

BY

GSRIBALASAITEJA GSRIKARTHIKEYA

 pencil

ISBN 978-93-5438-163-8

Published in India 2020 by Pencil

A brand of

One Point Six Technologies Pvt. Ltd.

123, Building J2, Shram Seva Premises,

Wadala Truck Terminal, Wadala (E)

Mumbai 400037, Maharashtra, INDIA

E connect@thepencilapp.com

W www.thepencilapp.com

DISCLAIMER: *The opinions expressed in this book are those of the authors and do not purport to reflect the views of the Publisher.*

Author biography

Introduction of the Authors

Teja and Karthik (Our short names)

This is our first book. We have poured **our hearts and soul** into this.

I am Sri Bala Sai Teja. G., 11 years old. I am born and brought up in Hyderabad. I have 4 members in family.

My birthday is on 20th March. My favorite subjects are Science and Math. Apart from Science and Math, I also love to study English as it is a very important and necessary subject for everyone across the world. My favorite food is any types of dishes made with chicken. When I grow up, I would like to be a doctor because it is my father's dream and I want to fulfill it. I am happy to take up this profession as it will let me help others. I am skilled at many sports activities like swimming, football, cricket, archery, running, karate, kabaddi, chess, carom, skating and badminton and am trained in these. I love to play cricket as it is my favorite game as well as my hobby. But my first priority is always studying. I always score more than 85% marks and be among the top 3 students of my class. I was awarded many academic and sports prizes since Nursery standard.

I am a very passionate guy and believe in self-learning. This self-learning made me a researcher also. I just started learning and working on research and development studies as well.

My email address: sbstm20@gmail.com

I am Karthikeya. G., 9 years old. I was born and brought up in Hyderabad. My birthday is on 23rd August. My favorite subjects are Science and Math. When I grow up, I would like to be a doctor to fulfill my father's wish. I am skilled at many sports activities like swimming, skating, football, cricket, archery, running, karate, chess, carom, kabaddi, and badminton. I love to play football too and this is one of my favorite games and a hobby as well. I am a football champion. But no matter what, my first priority is always studying. I always try to score more than 85% marks and be among the top 3 students of my class. I received many academic and sports prizes since Nursery standard.

I am a very passionate and strongly believe in self-learning. Through self-learning I could become a researcher and am working on research and development studies recently.

My email address: karthikeya2308@gmail.com

Wishing all my readers as well as everyone "Stay Healthy and Be Happy!"

Contents

Acknowledgements

Thank you!

Thank you for reading our book!
Thank you for your time.

Please send us your feedback, love letters (appreciations) and wholehearted blessings. That is all we ask for! Thank you.

Email address:

sbstm20@gmail.com
karthikeya2308@gmail.com

Teja and Karthik.

Introduction

This book is realistic in nature and the portrayals are made in a candid and vivid way. I was inspired to write this book from my experiences while growing up as well as the enriching knowledge that I gained from my father's story. This book deals with a broader concept and thus is relatable to both the kids and their parents.

This book basically tells about the hurdles of life that we all can face while accomplishing one's goals. In this book's content, I have tried to explain how we need to deal with the problems and create a wonderful journey toward success. It is true that every individual do not face the same kind of challenges. But on a broader picture, all the challenges are similar for all. Some points are listed as follows:

Be yourself and true to yourself : Don't get diverted listening to others words and ask your heart what you want to do the most.

Passion: Always think well, be good, and help others. Be passionate about your goals.

Mindset & Will power: Hone your skills to build up strong mindset and will power. Mindset first and keep the dependency as last option/alternative. **Monday to Saturday – Mind day, Sunday – Lazy day.**

Always be ready to welcome changes: Changes are inevitable so you must embrace changes with open arms.

Resilience and Reinvention: Train your brain to be unique and skillfully think about resilience and reinvention.

I think, for every problem there's a solution. If we don't have any solution, then it is not a problem at all!

I am sharing the real-life stories of my life, wonderful experiences, and key learning while being connected with my parents, teachers, and friends.

Happy Learning!

Contextual

One fine morning, my only sweet brother, Karthik, began to cry out loud at the very first hours of the day. Although it was too early for me to wake up, I still did as there was no other choice for me. My deep sleep was completely broken from the chaos that was going on in my house. When I woke up and rubbed the sleep off my eyes, I saw that all the lights in the room were turned on. Meanwhile, my parents were worriedly massaging Karthikeya to relieve him from his pain as he had a severe leg injury.

Seeing my brother's sorry condition, even my eyes became moist. I got up and joined my parents to help them in giving Karthik some medication immediately. Seeing him writhing in pain made me immensely upset as that day his regular routine was going to be missed. His daily routine was simple—to go in front of the mirror after waking up, neatly combing his hair, and finally coming to me with a huge smile lingering on his lips. I always adored seeing him like that.

Anyways, after quite some time, the pain seemed to have ceased a little and was under control. Dad asked Karthikeya to sleep for a while.

But my brother pouted cond said, "Dad I'm not feeling sleepy at all. Can you please tell some stories? I promise you Dad, if you tell me stories, I will surely go to sleep like a good kid."

I instantly asked the same and joined hands with my brother.

But Dad looked quite upset and said to us, "Kids, I am not in a good mood to tell stories today. I need to work and arrange some money to pay your school fees and medical expenses (X-ray, MRI and others things). I need to work hard children, please do try to understand."

We then meekly asked him, "Dad, can't we study at school without paying the fees?"

He smiled and showed me the school fee reminders and messages that were brimming in his inbox. He said, "It is known by all that if you don't pay fee, they don't allow us to be part of the school and we will also not be able to write in the exams. Paying the fees is must for the education and other holistic things that are being provided to us from schools. But to be honest, I don't see a proper and good education system which facilitates quality learning for people of any age group, caste, creed, religion and region. I always believe in providing right values to you and Karthik based on real-life experiences. This will help you."

We asked him, "You don't have money, but still you spend so much for our schools, tuitions, stationeries, and other academics and sports. Why? Please explain."

He kindly smiled at me and gave me an example of his dad—our grandfather.

Our grandfather said to my father, "I can never compromise for your education. Education is only best thing I can do for you. If you study well, I will give you whatever you want or you can even get it by yourself."

He also said some famous lines:

Maatru devo bhava

Pitru devo bhava

Aachaarya devo bhava.

This basically means "Respects to Mother, Father, and Guru. They are all forms of God."

"Guru?" we asked him. "Can I consider my teacher as Guru and my school as the Holy place of worship?"

He said, "Yes, why not? But you know the answer better than me based on your experiences."

Then he told us about his school days. All his masters, teachers stayed at the same place. They used to put extra efforts, sometime even during the night as well just to help our father and his friends to get more marks and be knowledgeable without expecting any benefit in return. They were pure from their hearts. They used to play a lot of games together and continued the healthy personal relationship for many years with great respect. His masters always used to strain their throats and felt pain because they wanted to create an impact on the value and importance of the concept. They went on with their preaching no matter how much their throats hurt. He had never been to the tuition. Hardly did they do homework. Everything was taught to them at the school only.

Their teachers never scolded them for their mistakes, but they used to make them understand their faults in a very positive way (it was like a laughing period not a feedback period) and created a very healthy environment, but this was an exception for Class 10.

We asked him, "Do you miss them today?"

He said, "I don't really miss them because there's no change in the respect that I have for them in my heart."

Thus, both of us were extremely influenced and impressed by our father's experience stories and decided to write this book.

Be yourself and true to yourself

I am (Teja) named as the most Intelligent and Smartest kid at my home, grandparents' place, and at my schools too. I am always very energetic all the time. I made my presence everywhere and everyone used to miss a lot all the time.

Here I will be sharing my real-life stories, wonderful experiences, and key learning that I gained from my parents, teachers, and friends.

I am blessed to enjoy the true love and affections of my parents. When I was growing up, at the age of 3 I started going to a playschool.

The first major experience of my life began on the first day of the school. When I had to leave my dad's hand to enter into the school premises, I had to become independent. But I always knew that my dad or my mom would come to pick me up. My parents used to tell me that the playschool is just like a home, and the only change that one see was that in playschool a child start leaning by playing. But in reality, the concept was totally different.

I went inside the classroom and sat on the bench. They gave me a small toy and asked me to sit and instructed me not move at all. The tone used by my teacher was totally different from what I hear from my parents. They made me sit at one place and I was not even supposed to move my hands also.

I desperately missed the freedom of my home and wanted to be myself. "Do this! Do that!" I was always being instructed. This created some bias in my mind and it was a continued gadget.

After some time, I made some friends but still was uncomfortable. It seemed I always had to do things forcefully.

After Nursery, Dad moved me to some other school.

But there was no change and all over again the same old story in a new wine bottle. The first few days, they forced me to be silent and then some activities began. Some I enjoyed and some I did not understand at all. I didn't know what to do. Most of the time, I found my teacher to be a bit strict to all of us and wanted to control us by giving some instructions which I really did not understand. I was happy to see the playing area, but no one allowed us to play happily.

One fine day, my teacher asked me, "1+1 equals to?" I was unable to answer and I really don't know the reason. So the teacher asked me many times but my answer remained the same. She became extremely angry, used a harsh tone, and scolded me. That was my first ever scary and pathetic moment.

I wanted to tell her, **"Teach me with love."** But I could not as I was just a child.

After some time, I completely could adopt to the school environment apart from one or 2 naughty things that I ended up doing often. It took me around 2 years to understand the methods of the school world. But as days passed by I started to miss myself more and more. At home, I could be myself but not at school. Most of the times, I had to nod my head and had to agree with whatever they told me in school. I could not convey to them my own choices. "You like ice cream? I do too." It was like this. They didn't give any importance to the parents' views. They didn't allow the parents to give us lunch box before/during lunch hours. I had to eat the food that my parents packed for me in the morning, which was colder and harder. I still recall the days when my mother stood outside my house gate to feed me warm food as soon as I stepped down from the school bus. In many situations, my dad was very unhappy that the school only thought of the parents when it required its payment for fees.

So my parents opted for an easy option that will help me in learning. They arranged for proper study time at home. I could practice reading, writing, hearing and speaking and it really helped me. At home my parents used to understand the situation and act accordingly, whereas in school it was different. As I was a very energetic person and loved sports, I demonstrated the same at school during the sports hours. But in return they said that I was hyper active. My father was angry on the teacher for demotivating.

One day my pencil fell down while writing. I got up to pick it up. My teacher saw that and instantly asked, "Why are you moving out of your place?" I said, "I am trying to pick my pencil up as it fell down." She didn't even bother to listen to me and scolded me mercilessly. At that moment I felt so sad and it even continued for almost 2 to 3 days. This affected me so much that my scores dropped too.

One day there was an annual competition in my school. I was excited and wanted to be a part of the cricket team. But they simply did not allow me to be a part of the team. I informed my father and he allowed me to play with my friends at home. My father encouraged me and my passion and made me join a summer camp. But here they put me in dance group which was not my cup of tea. Anyways, most of my annual day preparations were painful and shady memories of mine. Making us practice under the burning heat of the sun and immediately asking us to study again. Many times the school management announced the name of the selected people, but I was never in the list. These were very disappointing and disheartening situations for me.

I've struggled most of the time in trying to be who I wanted to be and always had to try to please others.

My father helped me to overcome the challenges that I faced. He always told me, "You just be yourself, you are unique. I will take care of the feedback. Just concentrate on being yourself."

Don't forget that you have your own talent.

Being yourself does not mean you are being selfish. It doesn't mean you don't care about others. Being yourself means you like who you are. Being yourself means living life how you want to live it, regardless of other people's opinions. And it means you respect yourself. If you love yourself, then only you will be able to love others.

"Do everything from your heart."

After that, I observed a great change in myself. I began to get many awards and academic appreciations.

I recall that once I got very less marks in math and I was so scared about it. Then my father and I came to attend the PTM. The teacher showed him the paper and my father acted very seriously. After returning home, he again said the same words, "Just relax yourself and take a deep breath." Then he asked me the reason of my poor performance. I said, "I cannot understand the concepts properly, so I made some mistake while hurrying to complete the exam on time."

I was always instructed by my parents that if we really don't know the answer or was not prepared about the topic, it can be considered and we can prepare much well for the next time. BUT MAKING A MISTAKE OUT OF NEGLIGENCE OR CARELESSNESS IN SPITE OF THOROUGH PREPARATION IS NOT ACCEPTABLE AT ALL. A lesson to be remembered throughout lifetime.

Being honest to your parents is also being yourself.

My parents are always proud of me for being honest to myself and to them, in fact to everyone.

They always said, "Proud of you my dear super big boy."

So always be true to your heart and listen to what it speaks to you. Take care of your passion and follow your dreams.

Passion. Always think good be good to help others

I am (Karthik) named as the most lovable and clever kid everywhere. I am very energetic all the time and am always clear on what I want.

One fine day during summer camp, my father was about to join me in a cricket coaching center. He already spoke to the coach. Then he came to me and said, "You are going to be part of the cricket summer camp."

I took a minute and informed my Dad, "I'm interested and passionate to play football/soccer and not cricket. Is it ok?"

He asked me once again, "Are you sure you want to be a football/soccer player?"

I said, "Yes!" He gave me a warm smile and immediately made me join the football/soccer coaching. I enjoyed every moment of the game and even played the matches with the seniors.

Then finally a day came when my school sports coach announced that I was the captain for the Football Interschool Competition. As soon as my school sports coach announced that, I was in the ninth cloud of happiness and my team congratulated me. I immediately shared this news with my father.

When I reached home, he just kissed me on the forehead and said, "I am proud of you super little boy."

And he also added, "You have to win this!"

So we played with all our might and we didn't even give them a chance to score a goal. We scored 3 goals and we were extremely happy to win the 1st prize in the Interschool Competition Championship.

We were the champions. Everybody started cheering me and called out my name, "KARTHIK… KARTHIK…!" My dad was extremely happy of the banana shots and that day we could not stop smiling.

My banana shots made him wake up at the middle of the night also!

Being declared as MAN OF THE MATCH was the most joyful moment of my life and it came to me as a surprise.

My brother captured this moment really well in my dad's mobile. I am so grateful to him and his photography skills.

Our team was declared as the winning team and we were awarded with medals and certificates.

I was also appreciated by the school principal. He said, "You are an excellent academic performer though being a new student."

I also had very similar challenges that my brother Teja had to face too, but we followed our parents' aphorism.

During the mid of the academic year, I was really disturbed by one of my classmates. We informed the school many times but no action was taken against him.

To be honest, although being in the school for one and half years, I could only learn to hold the pencil properly after being taught by the home tutor.

Sounds silly, doesn't it? But it's true.

I always was fond of dogs and wanted my dad to get me one puppy. Due to some or the other reasons, such as me being kid, its maintenance, hygiene etc., my dad always skipped that thought. But as it was my birthday wish, I got a chance to demand for it again. This time I was sure that they won't deny my wish as it was for my happiness. After few days, we got a small puppy. I selected it among many other puppies. Somehow I got connected to that little innocent cute puppy very soon.

After some formalities and few instructions, we brought my puppy home from the adoption center. I am clearly mentioning that it is from an adoption center, so it is not of any high-class breed. It's just a stray puppy whose mother was adopted by the adoption center people.

Though I had the chance to buy a high-class breed dog, I didn't go for it, because whenever I used to see a stray dog I would feel sad for it as they have no food, water, and shelter. So as dogs of classy breeds will be chosen by anyone, I wanted to give this stray puppy a family.

Finally on November 10th, we brought our puppy home and named it SIMBA. I am glad I am so glad to have adopted Simba. It showers all its love and affection on us. Simba is also very naughty and pretty much intelligent.

I would like to share an incident which happened at my school. It sounds so funny whenever I am reminded of the incident and my parents find it very cute .On the fifth day of my new school, we were supposed to have Hindi class. So as per the principal instructions, the teachers were supposed to check that every student has purchased their books for the academic year as we were supposed to get them online.

As the purchase was to be done online, some of my classmates didn't get the books on time though they have made the payments earlier. So they had to borrow books from the fellow students who could already buy the books in time. All the students who lend their books were appreciated. I too was one of them. As it was Hindi class, a sudden thought came in my mind and I said to my teacher in Hindi, "kar bhala to ho bhala." This to my teacher's and everyone's surprise was so apt at that moment. In the same way, we lend the books to them and after they get their own, they gave it back to us.

Kar bhala to ho bhala was my statement which was passed out of innocence and intelligence where I didn't even mean to get any applause in return. But this had such a deep connection to the situation.

But my teacher and classmates were so impressed at my thought that I was given a star on that day, which made me so happy.

Speak out whatever there is in your mind; be wise and brave.

Always be ready and welcome change

Karthik and I always go to my grandmother's place to play with Tapash (my nephew, mentally disabled kid). He can't play like us and he can't do the things like us because none of the schools welcomed him to be a part of the normal education system.

I asked my Aunty, "How to deal with this?"

She said, "I am so glad that that you asked me this question." Everyone in my family always encourages us to ask questions.

She said, "Bring change in Tapash. Welcome his world and make him welcome the changes in his life. It's just love and affection. This is going to be the real change in your life. Trust me."

Karthik and I enjoyed a lot being with Tapash as well. Sometimes when we sense difficulty, we ask my Aunty to deal with that. Today, he is an inspirational dancer. The best part is that he doesn't know the cheating game. He always plays a fair game. He offers everything to us except Burger and soda.

The bravery and change that you provide others replicate in your life in the future. Always accept change and encourage others to do the same too.

Change is a part of everyone's life. 'Keep moving' and 'keep changing' are the famous quotes I have heard since long. Adaptation to new horizons, new challenges, and new environment is always commendable.

That will make us to cope up and face life; however, when my parents told me that life is not always a "Bed of Roses" and we need to keep removing thorns and move on, I felt this was such an appropriate statement.

Maybe we want to welcome change with all out heart, but we are definitely sacred and tired of the adaptation that we need to go through if we accept change. So we need to be brave to accept change and must be prepared to deal with the hardships with a courageous heart.

Here are few instances of our lives where change is commendable and we have to welcome changes.

Change comes right from our birth; we adapt it, enjoy and accept. Changes are sometime uninvited too, for example, we may come across some illness, health issues which we are supposed to face, fight, and overcome.

Changes come in our way and help us to grow, to improve, and to develop so we must welcome these in a warm way.

Changes are directly related to adaptability.

I would like to share one of our experiences. We both have common experience as we are always together and there is not much age gap between us. We are hardly 1 year 5 months or so between us and so it seems like we are almost of the same age. Change and challenge from a newborn to a toddler to playgroup and primary section is seen year by year. Due to some unattended concerns, we had to change school where we both were at a stage when we resisted leaving our good old friends. But as we respect our parents' decisions and concerns for us, we moved to another school which was a great challenge. Though my dad has taken the decision, even he too was concerned about the change. But in a few days only, we have adapted to the changes and have adopted all the new rules of the school. This helped us to outgrow our fear of the new atmosphere and we were able to enter a new phase. This helped us turn each and every aspect into a joyous moment. We both were always appreciated for our performance—both in academics as well as extracurricular activities. We received much applause from our teachers and friends.

As a part of our co-curricular activities, we were engaged in karate. One day, to be precise one bad day, I (Karthik) got hurt pretty badly on my knee while performing karate. But somehow I managed to endure the pain and took some medicines and applied some ointments and few days passed by. But the pain had temporarily subsided; but it reoccurred on an instance and I had to make a drastic change in my daily routine.

I couldn't move, walk, and chill around like before. I was almost confined to my couch for most of the time. My playtime was cut down. Through these agitating days,

I started learning more about my condition. I searched Google and learnt many new things. In these mundane days, I comforted my heart by saying that it is good to spend time at home as the whole corona frenzy was going violent around the world.

And this is absolutely my positive approach to life. This is a must for everyone and one must understand that most of the times change helps you to look at the world with a different perspective.

CHANGE FOR A CHANGE IS ALWAYS ACCEPTABLE AND COMMENDABLE.

DO KEEP CHANGING!

Did I miss anything for accepting and welcoming change? No! But I really gained many things in return and also received self-satisfaction.

Mindset - Will power

We plan our Sundays as the best lazy day and this is my key for success. Sounds different, doesn't it? But it means a lot.

Every Sunday, I wake up whenever my stomach gives red signal and complains for food. When I wake up, I see the other two laziest people still sleeping. It's my Dad and Karthik!

One fine Sunday, my stomach was growling angrily. I woke up and just took a moment to think, what should I do now?

Should I wake my Dad up or should I sleep some more?

I then felt that waking up my Dad was the best option as I can't go back to sleep. By then my "jingle food bells" in my stomach was ringing loudly and thus these would not allow me to sleep! Although it's a difficult task, I didn't have any other option than to do so.

"Dad, please wake up," I said but he did not respond. After several pulls and pushes, he asked me, "What's the time?" I glanced at the clock and informed him, "It's 6 o'clock.

He just said, "Why can't you sleep some more? It is too early for us to wake up."

"Ok dad, I will sleep some more," I said. Again after some time, my stomach complained. I tried to wake up my dad up.

He again asked the same question.

I again informed that it was 6am.

He again grumbled and said that it was too early to wake up.

Now I had a doubt; why was the clock is showing the same time? I started my investigation and found that there was no battery inside the clock! It was removed by my dad last night. And I know that he did it because he wanted to set the lazy Sunday standard.

But still I asked him, "Why have you removed the battery?"

In return he gave me an innovative answer that he removed battery to generate electricity as there was no power at home last night.

We start hitting each other for some time till my stomach rang the danger bell again.

We tended not to do any other work in the weekends apart for completing my schoolwork and plan for next week for 30 minutes. Our motto was LET THE UNPLANNED BE THE RULER FOR A DAY! Everyone must enjoy both sides of the coin.

From this incident I also learnt that we must be independent and rely on the alarm of our minds and stop depending on materialistic things.

I make it a point not to miss my Sunday Laziness on every weekend because:

"Willpower is the single most important keystone which we must adopt as a habit for individual success. The major shift is your will power."

Flip sides of the coin always help us to gear up. Every day put yourself in a new challenging situation. But set yourself for failure every Sunday.

This shift and mindset planning will make you intelligent and help you to be successful.

Trust me, No one can compete with you at all.

Monday to Saturday: Plan your schedule in your mind. Keep the dependency things as last option/alternative. Just do for 3 weeks. Then see the magical transformation in yourself.

Did I miss my Sunday Laziness? Never! And same goes for you too!

Resilience and Reinvention

Here comes the most joyous phase of every child's life after a hectic and tiresome academic year.

My brother and I were planning for our holidays in the summer vacation. We engaged ourselves in sports. It's our passion. I loved cricket and my little brother loved football.

But here comes the twist in the tale, in fact villain of our story is CORONA.

Since many days we were hearing about some dreadful disease spreading all across the world. But somehow there was a sigh of relief in our country that this virus cannot sustain in our country in this extremely hot and humid climatic condition. They even said that this disease cannot spread in this country due to our food habits or the resistance power we possess.

But we received a shock one fine morning when we came to know about the pandemic corona entering in our country and everything started turning upside down! All our plans went in vain. I was pretty upset as the schools declared holidays, institutions were closed, sports centers were closed, and swimming as a part of summer vacation was completely ruled out. My birthday was near and I had planned so many things for the day. Though it was not a perfect birthday deal, but we were supposed to have fun with friends and family. The immediate day it was declared

Janata curfew throughout the country. Still there was no panic-stricken situation, but as the corona cases kept on increasing and were creating lot of tension and chaos in the country, there was lockdown announced to battle corona and the lockdown is being extended still.

With all these situations, our summer camp, our sports coaching, archery, karate and everything came to an end for the year. Our wishes were completely washed away. We were upset and angry with the current ongoing situations. But being resilient doesn't mean being good all the time! It means it fine to feel bad sometimes. There's a growing mental health crisis occurring right now. With the current pandemic, economic instability and unsure future, the rates of anxiety and depression are brimming to the fullest. To put it in a simple way, we are becoming less psychologically resilient.

Psychological resilience doesn't come from positive feelings. It comes from leveraging your negative feelings. It's the ability to take things like anger and sadness and make them useful and productive.

So we have taken corona as a challenge and channelized the worst to turn it into holidays which is somewhat life changing; this may not be the case for the elders but we as kids felt so.

So in a positive turn out, instead of sticking to gadgets in a playful way we have made them a weapon to achieve some useful skills.

We enrolled ourselves in some online courses, and I remind you again they are not some games.

As a part of our activities, we engaged ourselves in improving our communication skills in general topics, which according to us is pretty good related to our human body. I guess my dad intellectually gave the idea.

As a relaxation, he asked my younger bro to keep sending some funny topics related to our academics. I guess that's a smart move.

But you know what? We both loved it, as science is our favorite subject and our interest has grown day by day. We started learning new and interesting topics about human body and the physiology. We have learnt presentations. We have improved our body language. Whenever we used to perform our tasks to the fullest, we used to demand whatever we want. We both used to compete with each other, of course in a healthy way.

In the due course, we completed many online certified courses such as Google Smart Kid Beginner and Public Speaking Mastery . We have created our own email IDs and learnt many new things about handling net and system. We keep sending mails to our mom which we all enjoy.

We have enrolled online courses for different sports too, so that by the time begin again, we can learn every minor trick, hint, rule of the games.

We have planned to properly utilize my father's hard-earned money during the corona pandemic and were determined to achieve something good with it.

In this time of confinement, we are also enjoying my mother's home-cooked healthy meals which are so much better than the lavish dishes found in the restaurants.

We are also enjoying the time we can now spend with our family. You must enjoy it too! Stay at home and enjoy the company of your loved one.

Disclaimer This is purely my thoughts experiences not copied from any book or any source. Most of the things will not match as I tried to be unique and

Disclaimer

This is purely my thoughts/experiences not copied from any book or any source. Most of the things will not match as I tried to be unique and considered to be objective. Most of these are of my parent's knowledge/learning sessions and other form of my learnings.

I am a kid and in a learning stage and I know that there is a lot to learn. But I think that my experiences/situations will definitely connect to you all as we all face these situations. I will tell you about how to enjoy and create the path to be successful.

We advise readers to take full responsibility and clarification for your need by taking help of your parents and know their limits.

We can change our lives. We can do, have, and be exactly what we wish.

Together, let's look ahead at the bright future.